Luke Ba......

ALL WE EVER WANTED WAS EVERYTHING

OBERON BOOKS
LONDON

WWW.OBERONBOOKS.COM

First published in 2017 by Oberon Books Ltd
521 Caledonian Road, London N7 9RH
Tel: +44 (0) 20 7607 3637 / Fax: +44 (0) 20 7607 3629
e-mail: info@oberonbooks.com
www.oberonbooks.com

A catalogue record for this book is available from the British
Library.

PB ISBN: 9781786822482
E ISBN: 9781786822499

Cover image by Middle Child

Printed, bound and converted by
CPI Group (UK) Ltd, Croydon, CR0 4YY.

Visit www.oberonbooks.com to read more about all our books
and to buy them. You will also find features, author interviews and
news of any author events, and you can sign up for e-newsletters
so that you're always first to hear about our new releases.

ALL WE EVER WANTED WAS EVERYTHING

For /t/

*This play is for them, everyone who still believes
that things can only get better, and the people of Hull.*

This production would not have been possible without the following people and organisations:

Hull UK City of Culture 2017, Hull City Council, Arts Council England, Goodwin Development Trust, Hull Truck Theatre, Paines Plough, Humber Street Sesh, New Diorama Theatre, Henrietta Duckworth, Jack Chamberlain, Helen Goodman, Martin Atkinson, Martin Green, Lindsey Alvis, Durham Marenghi, Mark Page and Dan Mawer at Humber Street Sesh, Dav Forster and Mark Hall at Welly, Hull Box Office, Poor Boy Boutique, and Stewart Baxter at Warren Records.

First performed on 6th of June 2017 at The Welly, Hull before transferring to the Paines Plough Roundabout at the Edinburgh Festival with the following cast:

Leah Bryony Davies
Chris James Stanyer
Kimberley Emma Bright
Brian Joshua Meredith
Asteroid / Holly Alice Beaumont
The MC / Tom / Colin Marc Graham

Production Team
Writer Luke Barnes
Director Paul Smith
Composer / MD James Frewer
Producer Mungo Arney
Marketing & Communications Jamie Potter
Set & Costume Design Bethany Wells
Assistant Designer & Stage Manager Natalie Young
Sound Designer Ed Clarke
Lighting Designer Emily Anderton
DSM Sophie Clay
Movement Director Yassmin Foster
Assistant Director Josie Davies
Lighting Operator Jose Tevar
Sound Operator Matt Pilsworth
Dramaturg Stef O'Driscoll
Company Member Ellen Brammar
Company Member Matthew May
Company Member Edward Cole

This text is as it was performed in Hull, 2017, for Capital of Culture. For all future productions please feel free to amend any references to *where* the piece is being performed and *when*. The same goes for references to location: It is encouraged that it is tailored to *your* community and to *your* audiences.

Characters

Leah

Chris

Kimberley

Brian

Asteroid

Holly

The MC

Tom

Colin

One

The MC Hello Hull!

(A countdown starts on the screens, counting down to the beginning of the show.)

Are you ready?

PROLOGUE – TRACK 1a: 1987 // "OUR HEROES ARE BORN"
26th June 1987

(THE MC appears, halfway between a front man and a narrator. He is free to improvise and chat with the audience throughout. He is in this space with us, at this time, on this night.)

> I wanna dance with somebody
> 'Cos nothing's gonna stop us now
> There's no such thing as society
> And heaven is a place on earth

1987.
Shell suits and Mods dominate our retinas
And our TVs tell us that our terrorists are Irish

Two weeks ago Margaret Thatcher won her third election as Prime Minister. Our longest serving leader although no one here voted for her.

> The whole nation takes pity
> on Brian Horton's second division Hull City.

In Hull it's a wet Summer

> The smell of rain hangs like a memory as new life breathes into Hull.

But despite the rain giving an air of possibility Hull is full of negativity.

(The music shifts in tone, KIMBERLEY and BRIAN sing.)

And in a run-down and grey city centre hospital Brian and Cassandra are expecting their baby

And near them

Are Kimberley and Derek

And neither

At this point

Have any idea that their children will meet, or that their partners will disappear.

(BRIAN and KIMBERLEY sing the pain and worry of childbirth. Eventually, the children appear.)

BABIES!

Our heroes are born

(Our heroes appear, CHRIS and LEAH join in the singing.)

Chris, a well spoken young man with money, time for learning and hobbies, and Leah, brown haired and gobby waiting for a chance to be somebody

Meanwhile…

(A sudden cut in the music and we hear the beat of our ASTEROID for the first time. Our focus shifts to the space above.)

In the endless space above them, a comet races across the starry night sky. It screams directionless into the black and smashes into an asteroid, giving a birth of fire to it's own children.

(The asteroids are on fire in the sky.)

They watch over us

Paralysed in the night sky

Filling the darkness with order and light

And, in the middle, right in the middle of the new born cosmos, is *our* Asteroid…

(Then our ASTEROID appears. Masked. Making music. In glamour.)

…born into star dust and fire, standing supreme like a goddess in the night sky. And, like a goddess with the power of all the angels beating through her veins, she turns her naïve eye to the earth and all she can see is the endless possibility for humanity.

And with all the hope for life and love and laughter in her heart, she sings and we dance.

This is the City of Culture. This is theatre like you've never seen it before. This is *All We Ever Wanted Was Everything*.

PROLOGUE – TRACK 1b: "WE SING FOR YOU"

The Asteroid
We sing for you.
We sing for you.
We sing for you.
The stars are singing too
For your beating hearts
Are beautiful.
There's nothing you can't do.

(The night fades.)

TRACK 2a: 2007 // "COOL BRITANNIA"
Friday 30th May 1997

The MC Our story starts ten years after our heroes are thrown into the world without asking to be. 1997: Britpop, Blair and Mark Hateley's Hull City in Division Three.

(Ten years pass. The music has shifted in style, from the synths of the 80s to the guitars of the 90s. So too have the characters who now sport the fashion of the 1990s. We are now in 1997's Cool Britannia.)

The MC
Barbie Girls. Beetlebums.
More money and more problems
I believe I can fly
I believe I can fly
Believe I can fly
Believe I can fly
Believe I can fly

TRACK 2b: "THINGS CAN ONLY GET BETTER"

The MC Rumours are rife that the Good Friday agreement is near, And the press interest in Princess Di means that she lives in fear.

On the North East coast of Cool Britannia our heroes are now ten years old.

Him in a big house on the Avenues; her a smaller one on the other side of town that she's yet to outgrow.

They are as separate as kindness and hate although neither have learnt to do either yet.

(The music comes back in, with the underscore of "Things Can Only Get Better".)

(KIMBERLEY's House. KIMBERLEY and her son CHRIS enter. Her wearing 90s knitwear, him wearing a Euro 96 football shirt. He sits playing with his Game Boy. KIMBERLEY stands for a second watching him.)

The MC Sitting in the back room of her Avenues house with black coffee in a pot thirty year old Kimberley is about to tell her son Chris some news.

Kimberley I'm scared.
In my sleep I dream of my partner, eyes open; breathing and living with a whole life before him but when I wake he's in bed starting his departure to another world.
I'm a teacher but I don't know what to teach my son
How do I teach Chris to live a life now his dad's is done?
Chris.
Come and sit
There's something I need to tell you and I need you to be brave for a little bit.

The MC He knows she's going to say it

The fear lives in his shoulders like nits in hair

And young Chris realises his despair when he says:

Chris Is Dad –

Kimberley Yes.

Chris Ok.

The MC He doesn't know what to say.

All he can feel is a lightness in his legs

A head full of hay where there's no room for thoughts.

He is numb

Chris Was he in pain?

Kimberley No
No, he just breathed out
And that was that.

Chris What happened?

Kimberley He just went
No pain
He just closed his eyes
And
That was it.
Lost like tears in rain.

Chris Was it my fault?

Kimberley What?

Chris Am I being punished for not being good enough?

Kimberley By who?

Chris I don't know.
Dad.
God.

Kimberley No one's punishing you.

Chris Is it because I couldn't do my scales?

Kimberley No.

Chris What's cancer?

Kimberley It's a disease
It appears anywhere
(On your dad it was his tummy)
And then wraps itself around the body
And one by one
The body just…
Dies.
But don't worry he didn't cry he just…left.
I'm sorry darling, is this upsetting you?

Chris What happens now?

Kimberley Come here.

(They embrace.)

Our ancestors are watching
As we burn our fires
Brighter than what came before
Brighter than they ever saw
They say things can only get better
Things can only get better
Things can only get better
Things can only get better
They say

Chris What happens now?

Kimberley What happens now is
We live
You and I we give all we can
And we throw ourselves into it.
We don't hold back one bit
For Dad
Ok?

Chris Ok.

Kimberley Chris. This is your chance to do something.
Now I have a house and money I don't have to worry
That's what Dad would have liked
Daddy grew up with nothing you know, he had to get on his bike
He went to university and he was the first one in his family
You could go too.
But you have to work, ok boo?
Deal?

Chris Deal.

Kimberley Ok baby.
You can do anything.
If you can dream it, you can do it.
You just have to work.
Come on.
Let's start with the piano.

(CHRIS goes to the piano.)

Make Daddy proud Chris.

(*BRIAN's house. BRIAN enters, wearing a black bomber jacket.*)

The MC Brian is a thirty year old man of masculinity and muscle

He found his way to being a bouncer in the hustle and bustle of Hull City centre by twatting Jon Pringle when he said he looked like Ken Dodd on the quad in Year 8.

Ever since that day he's been brimming with hate.

It lives inside his shoulders and comes out in his hands that lash out with the weight of boulders.

Brian started fighting fights for people who could not stand up to bullies.

And although he's fully aware of the violent world he's in, he took the path of the righteous fully.

He became an angel.

The natural progression: a bouncer with the weight of the world in his heart

And as time goes on he starts to wonder what else there could have been if he'd been given the start

And even though what he was given was shit

He thought he'd better try and make the most of it

So he got a family

And then his wife left him.

Brian I'm bored
In my dreams I soar above rainbows and unicorns
I throw pound coins on fucked up bagheads tangled up in thorn bushes and I laugh at their pain.
But I can't laugh for long because really we're the same.
Them hooked on drugs and me relying on who sells them in L.As to make money.
I can't work computers.

I'm not being funny but when would I have had the chance to learn
that when I've had to put food in my daughter's tummy?
Buy toast. Buy honey.
For Leah.

(LEAH appears in a Geri Halliwell Union Jack dress, scribbling on her
trainers.)

Leah Are you going out again tonight Daddy?

Brian Yes darling, you know Daddy's got to work.
It makes me sad to know that I don't get to tuck her up at night
Her mum a fuck up in her own right
Out getting fucked up to ignore the clock ticking on her own mortality.
And to be honest, I wish I was too, but for her I have to keep my sobriety.
I wish I had the balls to do what I should do and fuck off
Leave Leah in some home with two toff foster parents in sweaters
My betters
Send her away to a life of books and art galleries and plays.
But no way. I'm better than that.
I want nothing more than for her not to be me.
I only hope she can see how much that would mean to me.

Leah Daddy?

Brian Yeah?

Leah Holly took the piss out of my trainers

Brian They're vintage.
Tell her to shut up.
You can't let girls like that keep you up at night.

Leah Holly's dad's got a car.

Brian We've got a car.

Leah No, we've got a car they've got a *car* car
Like one that's more impressive by far.

Brian Our car's impressive.
It's a 2CV.

Leah Theirs is an Audi.

Brian So what?

Leah So that's cool.

Brian A 2CV is cool!

Leah It's not Dad.
She's got a satellite TV and a computer with the internet
It's not fair.

Brian You've got ya Spice Girls dress.

Leah I know, it's the best.
But I want to go to music classes
And ballet
And have fun.
Ride horses.
Do stuff.
I want to be like Holly.

The MC And Brian doesn't know what to say
What can you say to a child who wants what you can't give them today?

Brian Look. I'll never be like Holly's dad.
But that doesn't mean that you will never have all that.

Leah What do ya mean?

Brian In a long line of people that have lived here and worked on boats
And in factories making coats
You're the first one that can go to university
Or do whatever you want
If you take advantage of this opportunity.
Things are changing
You could live a life better than Dad.
Live a life doing that.
Get a house, a proper job, a cat.
You can do anything you like
You kids can get on your bikes.
Look up.
All the ancestors you have are looking down on you
These are the same stars they saw in the same place like glue.

You're sharing the night with the fisherman and factory workers
and farmers
And they're saying:
The good times are coming
You can be whatever it is you want to be
If you work hard enough.
I've got to go to work, Nan'll be here in a minute.
You going to do your homework?

Leah Yes.
I'm going to do everything I can.

Brian Good girl.
Give us a kiss.

(She kisses him on the cheek.)

>   *Our ancestors are listening*
>   *Their ghosts are in the walls*
>   *Telling us all to rise up*
>   *And to take our place in the stars*
>   *They say things can only get better*
>   *Things can only get better*
>   *Things can only get better*
>   *Things can only get better*
>   *They say*

Brian Good night.

The MC And Brian steps out into the night

Into the land of peaches and cream, hoping to God there won't be a
fight, not tonight

Just the usual girls in dresses split at the seams and boys off their
tits on pills to escape their drifting dreams.

Bomber jacketed at the door of Lexington Avenue Brian prays he's
right about his daughter.

And that the promise he made her won't come back to haunt her.

In her bed, Leah dreams of a life

Where she takes her kids to stables in a jeep and she's her own
Queen not some King's wife

And she laughs at all the sheep that have to work.

But she knows

Deep down in the pit of her stomach

As she lies in her single bed with the window that looks out onto
rows and rows of lock ups

That will never be her

They say things can only get better
Things can only get better
They say

TRACK 3: "YOU AND ME"
Thursday 26th June 1997

(Virgin Megastore, Princes Quay.)

(BRIAN and KIMBERLEY enter, him in the same bomber jacket as before – her wearing a different outfit from C&A.)

The MC A few weeks later and the sun is setting like the career of Tony Hawk, Pro Skater

Brian and Kimberley, separately, find themselves on the top floor of the new Virgin Megastore in Prinny Quay amidst the VCRs and CDs.

Looking for the last copy of a new book they've been told their kids should read

(They both reach for the last copy of 'Harry Potter And The Philosopher's Stone'. BRIAN just about gets there first.)

Brian Sorry.

Kimberley Oh it's fine.

Brian It's not for me.

Kimberley Well it wouldn't matter if it were for you.

Brian Wouldn't it?

Kimberley No.

Brian I was just saying.

Kimberley You can read Harry Potter if you like.

Brian Yeah but I'm not.

Kimberley Ok.

Brian I'm not reading Harry Potter.

Kimberley *(Finding him funny.)* Alright, I believe you. Who's it for?

Brian My daughter. It's her birthday today.

Kimberley Oh right.

Brian Yeah. Do you want it?

Kimberley Sorry?

Brian The book, do you want it?

Kimberley Oh no I couldn't.

Brian Na it's fine, honest. Here.

(He gives her the book.)

Kimberley Why you giving it to me?

Brian Dunno. My daughter doesn't even know she's getting it. She won't miss it.
Seriously, take it.

Kimberley I -

Brian Honestly I'll just come tomorrow.
It's on the way to work. Sort of.
Bet your…

Kimberley Son

Brian Yeah I bet your son is desperate for it, like honestly take it.

Kimberley Ok. Thanks. It's his birthday today too, so...thank you.

The MC Every ounce of Brian's body is burning with opportunity, this is great.
He's got to make the move before it's too late.

Brian Do you wanna go on a date?

Kimberley Sorry?

Brian Do you wanna go for a drink?

Kimberley Er... My husbands just died.
Cancer.
And I don't want to like, date.
I just want to concentrate on making the best life for my son.

Brian Yeah I know. I'm not hitting on you. I just meant a play date.
I want the same for my daughter
My wife left me for a hotel porter
And I don't want that for Leah
So my life is now for her.

Kimberley Right.
Although something about him tells me I should run away
I think I'm being unfair.
He's a person buying books for his girl
Maybe in a sea of pollution he's a pearl.
We should give people chances shouldn't we?
Yeah.
Why not.

MC She takes out her Nokia 5110 and gives him her number, which - not having a mobile - he writes down.

Brian I'll give you a call.

Kimberley Sure
Leah could do with a little friend.

Brian It's a date.

Kimberley A *play* date.

Brian Right, yeah, a play date.
See ya. I've gotta run up to Top Deck, get some clothes for the little one.

Them and us. You and me.
It does not do to dwell on dreams
and then, then forget to live
*

TRACK 4: "WATCH THE SUN TOGETHER"
Saturday 30th June 1997

(KIMBERLEY's house. A few days later. BRIAN enters KIMBERLEY's house tentatively, holding hands with LEAH. He has clearly made an effort, wearing a shirt. KIMBERLEY has also made an effort but not as obviously as BRIAN. The kids wear kids clothes.)

(They all sit, awkwardly.)

The MC A few days later they meet on their play date

Brian finds Kimberley's house on the Avenues to be beautiful

But is slightly put off by the pictures of her dead husband on the wall

Brian does not feel at home.

And Kimberley feels uneasy about having a man in her house for the first time since her husband died

The kids wait to be told to go and play

As their parents sit and drink coffee absolutely not sexually

Just let me in, let me in
Let us dance for tomorrow
Oh let me in, let me in
Let's watch the sun together

Brian Her house is massive and it makes me feel like a mong
Not like because I've done anything wrong
But because I'm singing from a different song sheet.

I'm ashamed. I'm standing shuffling my feet to hide the pain of not knowing what to say.
I'm a thug with half a brain and she's got a doctor for a dead husband that paid for all this.
Right kids, go and play.

(The kids rush off.)

(Upstairs.)

The MC Leah and Chris put foot after foot on the exposed wood staircase to look at something that makes Leah feel as out of place as a shoe lace in a box of worms.

His bedroom is as big as her living room

And the smell, to her, feels exotic. It's lavender. Although she doesn't recognise it.

And out of the window she sees trees

A myriad of impossibilities is all she sees in this house.

The parents downstairs as quiet as a mouse.

(CHRIS empties his school backpack of all of his toys – Pogs, wrestling figures, his 1997 Premier League sticker book and swapsies as well as school work, the Harry Potter book and a lunchbox. He looks at LEAH expectantly.)

Chris What do you want to play first? Do you have any swapsies?

(LEAH ignores him as she is fascinated with his dream wall.)

Leah What's this then?
It's bigger than Big Ben.

Chris This is my dream wall
One day I'm going to do them all.

Leah What's that?

Chris That's my main dream.
To be a psychologist.

Like my dad.
I want to help people that are sad like my mum.
I want to help people get off their bum and do stuff.

(Downstairs.)

Brian You like football?

Kimberley Not really. Watched the Euros last year.

Brian Yeah. Gareth bloody Southgate, eh!

Kimberley Yeah.

(Upstairs.)

Leah What does a psychologist do?

Chris Sit and listen.
That's what Dad says.
Said.
Sorry I'm not used to saying said.

Leah That's ok. Is he dead?

Chris Yeah.

Leah Why aren't you sad?

Chris Dunno
Too much to do to be sad.
Gotta be good because I don't want my life to be bad.

Leah Have you cried?

Chris No.
Don't want to
Just going to work.

Leah Do you work really hard?

Chris Yeah.
Do you?

Leah Yeah.

Chris What do you want to be?

Leah I don't know.

Chris Well, what do you like?

Leah I dunno.

Chris Why don't you know?

Leah No one's ever asked me.

Chris What's your favourite thing in the whole world?

Leah Animals
Ones that don't bite
Or fight
Or make too much noise.

Chris My favourite animals a bobcat.

Leah What's that?

Chris It's a big cat
Eat's things
And all that.

Leah Right.
I love dogs.
I think when I get a dog I'll cry a river.
I'd feel less lonely with something to pet.
Maybe I could be a vet

Chris Quite hard being a vet.
You'd have to work really hard.

Leah I will. Can I put it on the dream wall?

Chris Alright.
Go on.

(She does.)

Leah Do you think it'll come true?

Chris I hope so. If you can dream it, you can do it. That's what mum says.

Leah Shall we get married?

Chris What?

Leah Like shall we get married and then you can be a doctor and I'll be a vet, we can get a house and a dog and babies? I think life would be easier if we did it together. I'm just being practical.

Chris You wanna get married?

Leah I just think it would be a good idea to nab you down because you're obviously going to be successful.
We could be double rich if we did it together.
I'm just gonna ask you.
Will you marry me?

Chris Alright.

The MC Leah and Chris prepare their teddies for the service and as they do, downstairs another union is happening.

(Downstairs.)

Brian Do you get lonely, since…?

Kimberley Sometimes

Brian Me too.

Kimberley Right.

Brian Yeah. It's hard.

Kimberley Yeah.

Brian It's being older I think, because you think there's no one left.

Kimberley No.

Brian No one left to… Anyway.

Kimberley Yeah. I understand.

Brian Do you?

Kimberly I do.

(*BRIAN* kisses her. She kisses him back. Then, feeling guilty – she pushes him off.)

Na na na na na na na na na na
Na na na na na na na na na na

Kimberley What are you doing?

Brian What?

Kimberley You kissed me!

Brian I thought that's what you were saying

Kimberley Jesus Christ. No! My husband's just died. For fuck's sake.

Brian Oh Jesus, this is so embarrassing. I'm sorry.

Kimberley Get out.

Brian Yep fair enough.

(*He rushes upstairs to the kids.*)

Right Leah, time to go.

Chris I don't want you to.
Can she stay over?

Kimberley Chris!

Leah We're getting married.

Chris Can we hang out every weekend?

Kimberley We'll see.

Brian Well, they could do.

Kimberley We'll see.

Brian What's the problem?

Kimberley Nothing's the problem… I'll call you.

Brian … Come on sweetie.

(He takes LEAH's hand and they leave.)

Chris Can Leah come round again?

Kimberley I think it's best we get you some nice friends
From the tennis club
Or something
Ok?
Now go and wash your hands, dinner's nearly ready.

(Outside.)

The MC Outside Brian and Leah sit in the car listening to her All Saints tape and sharing a Kit Kat, knowing there's a long way to go before they will feel like they belong in houses like that.

Brian You have a nice time?

Leah Yes! Can we hang out again?

Brian I hope so.
Come on
Daddy's got ya
Let's get some oven baked smilies and peas.

> *Just let me in, let me in*
> *Let us dance for tomorrow*
> *Oh let me in, let me in*
> *Let's watch the sun together*

TRACK 5: "WAKE UP WHEN DREAMS ARE OVER"

(Two bedrooms: one Chris's, one Leah's.)

The MC In bed the two of them hug and read.

Parent and child; that feeling of safety that can only come with the other, like pulling a duvet up to ya face in a storm

Not knowing quite what to do with their children mum and dad drive themselves insane

Paralysed by their own failures

All of them eyes closed

And none of them

Looking at the sky.

At the asteroid that hears the song of humans: you succeed or you die.

The Asteroid
There's nothing left but sleep now.
Just darkness in the dark
There's no one left to hear now
The stars shine in the park
Hearts, wake up when dreams are over.
Hearts, wake up when dreams are done.
Hearts, wake up when dreams are over.
Hearts, wake up when dreams are done.

Chris I'm going to be great you know. For you.

Leah I love you Daddy.

(The parents and children embrace and drift off to sleep.)

Two

Monday 25th June 2007

(Ten years pass. The sights and sounds of Britpop give way to Indie guitars and skinny jeans. Brown replaces Blair and Britain is fighting alongside America in the 'War on Terror'. We are now in 2007's Broken Britain.)

The MC
Starz in our eyes
So shut up and drive
With all my friends
Time to pretend
What's done is done and
la da da
Our time has come ah
ha ha ha

Ten years later. Hull. 2007.

It's summer in Broken Britain and indie kids sit outside the newly built St Stephen's shopping centre wearing skinny jeans, playing The Kooks and wanting to go to the seaside.

Everyone's starting to look like clones with the launch of the very first iPhone. Gordon Brown is 48 hours away from becoming Prime Minister and Phil Brown is just months away from taking Hull City to the Premier League for the first time. Big Brother and The X Factor infect our streets with dreams of fame, and after 9/11 and 7/7 the War on Terror leads to fire and flame.

Chelsea Daggers
And paper planes
Big girls don't cry
You're so naïve
What's done is done and
la da da
Our time has come ah
ha ha ha

We return to our heroes as they turn twenty. Chris worked as hard as he could and made his way to Manchester Uni to study psychology

He thought he could be like his father but with the pressure his mum puts on him it couldn't be further from the truth.

In the biology of his body, the anxiety is crippling

But he won't let anyone see the chinks in his armour of masculinity.

And as he sets off to go home for Summer he can feel himself tipping over the edge.

> *What's done is done and*
> *la da da*
> *Our time has come ah*
> *ha ha ha*

Back home Leah

The girl with no dreams, let alone a dream wall

Works harder than anyone's ever worked in all of Hull

She breaks her back trying to do well

She stresses

The late nights cause crinkles in her eyes worse than the piles of unironed dresses

Her sweat turns to Red Bull

And when results day comes her heart is full

She's nervous

Hoping that one of the perks of her efforts will be a bright future

But opening the brown envelope it's clear her future is one of retail service.

With straight Ds it's unlikely she'll ever be given a proper chance.

She gets a job in Build-a-Bear a couple of hours at a time to fill her purse

She makes friends and they drink so much at weekends they burst.

She lives at home where her dad makes her clothes clean and she's so comfy and at ease in her routine she doesn't feel the need to dream.

And all the time the Asteroid is watching.

Falling out of love with the loveless world she sees below.

TRACK 6b: "I DREAM OF YOU"

The Asteroid
Last night I dreamed a dream of you
Of fire and of flame across land and sea
Last night I dreamed a dream of you
And burning homes of people no one knows
Planes crashing into land
Robots killing in sand
People crying death
And counting coins
I dream of you.
I dream of you.
I dream of you.
(Building intensity.) The stars are dreaming too
Of your breaking hearts
Once beautiful.
With your breaking hearts
There's nothing you can't do.

TRACK 7: "RAINBOWS, SPIDERS, VULTURES"

(KIMBERLEY's house. She sits drinking a glass of red wine, wrapping an iPhone 1 and the final Harry Potter book for CHRIS' birthday.)

The MC In the John Lewis kitchen of her house on the Avenues, Kimberley sits with a glass of red wine waiting for her son to come home. She's nervous despite speaking to him almost daily on the phone.

Kimberley Chris is back from uni for his birthday and I am ruining the oven making chicken.
I've got the lot: all his favourites right down to the turnips and roast potatoes with horseradish to dip in.
I'm so proud of him
He's heading for a first & he's always had a thirst for knowledge
I'm ashamed I never did enough with my life
I was a wife but I had the potential to do more than cut food with a knife.
I guess that's the thing us parents are scared to tell our kids
We're jealous that they're better than us.
They have more opportunity; less fuss
An easier life.

The MC Outside Chris is waiting
Breath baited he stops before he goes inside,
taking a moment before he steps into the tide.
He's sweating

A tension in his chest and his throat tightens as he's betting with himself how quickly his mum will ask how he's doing with his adventure at university.

Rainbows

Spiders

Vultures

All inside me

They twist and they turn

They rub and they burn

They smash and grab

They fuck and stab

Chris Ok.
I don't know what to say
Because
Because
Because
I
fucked
uni.
Not because I've been out on the mandy covered in uni-glow
Everything is sweet like fucking candy it's just that...
I don't know how to say it
I've never...
Ok...
I work FUCKING hard
And I really do
I'm not just saying that
It's just...
I'm not actually very bright.
And that mixed with the promised joy my mother gave me makes me lose sleep at night.
So convinced that she gave me the gift of not having to fight for anything I wanted.
How do you tell someone who's invested all their life in you
That you're actually not worth it.
In a small town it's easy to be king, hands down
In the big sea all ya do is drown.
I'm a mess
And it's best if I don't tell her because she'll kill herself
Find her swinging from the rafters
And she'll see me and before she dies she'll say "there's Penguins in the fridge for afters"
And to be honest that might be best for me
I'd inherit a house and could go through life worry free
Without the burden of mortgages or paying the rent and just be me.

The MC He takes a deep breath

And stands with his chin on his chest

Knowing it's best

To lie

To save his mother from moving from an angel on earth to one in the sky.

Chris Hi

Kimberley Hello Darling. Happy Birthday!

(She gives him the wrapped presents.)

So good to see ya looking so fresh.

How are ya?

Chris Aye good.

Kimberley How's uni?

Chris You know how uni is Mum, ya ring me every day.
She calls me asking if I've made the most of the 3k a year she's shelling out

Kimberley I know, but I'm just curious.

Chris Yeah it's going great.
It's not going great
I hate the feeling of my mediocrity burning up inside me.
Her happiness depends on me to be the man she wants to see.
Look at her
She's making me roast chicken with all the trimmings because she's proud.
How can I tell her I'm not the man she wants me to be.
I'm not intellectually endowed.

Kimberley I've bought ice cream.
Tell me everything
I'm so excited I could scream.

The MC And as she sits down on the leather couch
The smell of lavender overwhelming
Chris crumbles inside.

(The chorus repeats and intensifies under the following, closing in on CHRIS.)

Chris The feeling wraps about my shoulders
It puts boulders into my tummy and makes me feel funny.
My palms are sweaty
Knees weak arms are heavy but there's no spaghetti just fucking
pressure
And the pressure
This is no good for me
This is
This
Th
T

–

I've
Rainbows
Running

–

I

–

Cats

–

This too shall pass
Thi
This too shall pass
Thi
Th
This too shall pass this too shall pass this too shall pass this too shall
pass this too shall pass this too shall pass this too shall pass this too
shall pass this too shall pass this too shall pass this too shall pass this
too shall pass this too shall pass this too shall pass this too shall pass
this too shall pass
Fuck
Ok.
Breathe.
Rainbows.
Spiders.
T
T
Vultures
T

–

This too
Thi
Ti
T
Rainbows.
Spiders.
Huh.
Huh.
Huh.

Kimberley Dinners ready.
Why don't you come and tell me all about uni
And your plans for the future
I've been dying to hear for months just mooching about here.

Chris Yes Mum.
I'd love to.
And I sit down
To a tea of roast chicken with all the trimmings
And I imagine telling her everything.
how I've failed
how I'm not special
how I'm average
how I'm not going to be the man she wants me to be because I'm just normal.
But I don't say all that.
I tell her everything's fine.
Even though I spend all my time telling myself that I'll never be as good as Dad
And next to him everything I achieve will always look bad
I'll never be able to get anywhere near what she expects
It's the pressure from her that's made my life so complex
And to make things worse I've got to go out tonight for my birthday.
Dressed as a Disney princess.

Yes Mum. Everything's great. Really great. I'm really happy.

(*CHRIS unwraps the presents, loves his new iPhone and doesn't seem as bothered by the Harry Potter book. He smiles, hugs his mum and then gets dressed up as Pocahontas.*)

TRACK 8: "NIGHT FALLS"

The MC Night falls

Chris steps out as a Disney princess

And Leah steps out ready to spend her excess cash.

Both

   In a way

      Wearing costumes.

         The air is palpable

            The sun lingers too late.

               And there is sex in the air.

        Night falls
        Save me
        Night falls
        Hold me.

        Let me in your arms
        When night falls
        I just wanna be free
        I can feel your charms
        When night falls
        Together we'll be free
        Fall with me

(In Hull's Sugar Mill nightclub.)

Leah It's my birthday and I'm feeling a bit sweaty
This bras too tight on my back and I can feel my tits popping out of
it but despite that I'm happy with my life.
I've got friends, a family and generally speaking I'm not a cunt.
I'm in Sugar Mill for its reopening with the crew from Build-a-Bear
There's Sophie with the pigtails and Josie whose too pissed to get
up from her chair.

Everyone likes me because I've got energy like a bunny
I'm the best at work at like being funny

I have absolutely no problem with the rest of these wannabe wags
In their super high heels and their Gucci bags.
I learned that life is about living not getting
So I don't spend any time fretting about not going to university or leaving home.
Then as I'm smoking me last fag before the ban kicks in
Someone walks in who nearly makes me shit
It's Holly, my head girl; Holly Moffit
The one who scoffed at my trainers at school
And the worst thing is
I still want to be her mate because she's so fucking cool.

Holly Happy Birthday
You look gorge.

Leah She's seen my badge.
She says it like she knows my name
When she's clearly forgotten how she used to bully me in her mascara and her push up bra from Zara.

Holly I'm sorry do I know you?

Leah I knew she wouldn't recognise me.
It's me Leah

Holly I'm sorry I don't know.

Leah It makes me sick to think that I've got to explain myself
Was I that much of a gimp?
It's me Holly
From school

Holly Oh yeah. Hi.

Leah What have you been doing?

Holly Said fuck it to men, got a job and made a fuck ton of cash. How have you been?

Leah Fine yeah. Good. Great yeah. Just out partying. Just doing the partying thing at the moment. Having fun. Shagging lads. Yano. You?

Holly Partying? You still do that? More to life than getting fucked yano babes.

Leah Ano yeah I should grow out of it really
But it's my birthday so I'm out on a mad one, what you doing?

Holly Just came out for a laugh yano.
I've got some mates over from work and thought I'd show them all the shit places I used to go.

Leah This isn't shit.
This was Waterfront! It's where I had my first kiss with Tommy Grogan
This room is full of memories and she is taking the piss

Holly You can't still come here, like, seriously?

Leah I come here every week.

Holly Oh. Do you work near here?

Leah I don't want her knowing I build bears
I love it
But she'll think I'm shit
Sometimes there's no harm in lying just a little bit…

I work in a bank
I'm a banker wanker

She sucks her straw and looks around the dance floor for the nearest man she can ridicule
She is so fucking cool.
Then the most embarrassing thing happens since I wet my knickers in school.

DJ Shout out to the Build-a-Bear massive! WAHHHOOOOOOO!

(There's a cheer from the Build-a-Bear massive.)

Holly Ew

Leah Ano yeah. How tacky.

Holly Can you imagine working in Build-a-Bear?!

Leah Nah

Holly Wouldn't you hate building bears all day though.

Leah Dunno. I mean *I* would. But some people might not.

Holly I think it's shit. What'll happen when ya look back when ya old and haven't got a pension and spent ya whole life building bears.
People like us were built to make serious money.
But they're fucked; they're working in Build-a-Bear
They've got no chance of doing anything.

Leah In my mind I'm thinking why do you think you can talk about people like that?
Why do you think it's okay to talk down to people ya twat?
But she's so cool
And she does have a point
And I really want to be her mate.
so…

Yeah. Yeah I guess you're right.
Bear building pricks.
What do you do then?

Holly I work in energy over in Leeds
I match people up with energy deals
We're looking for more staff actually, I could sort you out if you like?
The money's great.

Leah Oh right
I'd love to
But I've got yano
The bank.
The wank bank.
That's what we all call it.
Everyone at the bank.

Holly Fair
Anyway, I've got to go.
If you want a hook up for that job let me know.

(They exchange numbers. LEAH notices that HOLLY has an iPhone.)

Leah Ok.

Holly You wanna join us for a drink?

Leah Yeah, might as well.
I play it cool but fuck me, I've been waiting for this moment my whole life.
Sorry girls. Just nipping the loo.
I'll be back... Soon.

(She disappears into the night.)

(In the Barracuda toilet's.)

The MC Chris sits in the bathroom of Barracuda examining his face in the mirror

So far from getting the life he wanted, aware his prospects are getting dimmer.

He's paralysed with fear.

Dressed like a Disney princess with the moment of his total failure, near.

> *Night*
> *Falls*
> *Save*
> *Me*
> *Night*
> *Falls*
> *Hold*
> *Me.*

> *Let me in your arms*
> *When night falls*
> *I just wanna be free*
> *I can feel your charms*
> *When night falls*
> *Together we'll be free*
> *Fall with me*

> *Fall with me*
> *Darling, fall with me*
> *As night falls*
> *As night falls*

Chris I'm here because they made me come out for my birthday. Even though I'd rather be curled up with Harry Potter seven like I'm still eleven

I'm wearing this fucking…
This…
Fuck it.

The MC Chris steps out into the pub

And in the hustle and bustle of fists and pheromones

He sees them all; his high school bros sitting in drag

Sipping on pints

This is his moment to sing in rhythm and rhyme.

He puts his fake smile on: showtime.

> *All the lads have all the banter*
> *All the lads have all the laughter*
>
> *All the lads have all the banter*
> *All the lads have all the laughter*

Tom Yes mate.

Chris Alright little man, how's it going?

Tom Are you PocahonTITS?

Chris I'm whatever you want me to be baby.

Tom You gonna neck me?

Chris Ha. No. Fuck off. Buzz Lightyear?

Tom Yes!

Chris Not a princess is it little man.

Tom No but it's funny innit.

Chris Yeah it's funny but he did say princesses so…

Tom Alright.

Chris I have nothing to say to these idiots that stayed at home
Just got to sit back and let them moan about their stupid little lives.

(Silence.)

What you been up to?

Tom Oh yano life.

Chris Good answer that

Tom What do you mean?

Chris People really mean like whats ya job, are ya married, how much sex you having. Fuck that life is like… Yano the living bit.

Tom Yeah. Works boring.

Chris Yeah?

Tom Yeah.

Chris What's ya job then?

Tom What?

Chris Ya job what's ya job?

Tom Just in an office
Insurance

Chris Sound. Did you not fancy leaving Hull?

Tom No.

Chris Right.

Tom How's the sex life?
Must be fucking wild at uni?
Are you just drowning in fanny?

Chris Yeah. Loads
I can't be arsed anymore
Like literally can't be arsed shagging.
My dicks red raw.

Tom How is uni?

Chris Yeh mate. It's the fucking dream. I honestly pity anyone that hasn't been.
That's not what I want to say.
I want to tell him how his mediocrity makes me sick because he hasn't even tried.
I want to tell him how little I give a fuck about anyone here.
I want to tell him that he is every woman in this rooms last resort.
I want to tell him that him not trying is even more disgusting than me not succeeding.

But I don't.

I pick up my pint

And I drink

I have the banter

I laugh at the shit jokes

I listen to the stale stories

I be a lad.

And I wish I could go home and read.

But I don't

Because when you're a man there's a certain life you have to lead

This is my life now. I'm not moving anywhere else with my grades. I'll just be here doing…something. So I've got to learn to enjoy it.

Come on Tom. Let's do what we do best. Let's get fucked.

(And they do, joining in with the following chorus like a bunch of lads.)

Night falls
Save me
Night falls
Hold me.

Let me in your arms
When night falls
I just wanna be free
I can feel your charms
When night falls
Together we'll be free
Fall with me

TRACK 9: "DRIFTING AWAY"

(After closing.)

Drifting away
We're drifting apart
We used to be closer way back when
I'm ready to soar without you near

The MC After the clubs close all that's left is the alien music playing from kebab shops and shouting.

The boys and girls shivering waiting for taxis wishing they weren't going home alone

This is where the image of life is projected

But where no living happens

For others there's the conversation

With housemates

With lovers

Or, as in Leah's case, with parents.

And these conversations change lives.

Like this one

With Leah and Brian; him interrupted from playing Pro Evo as she crashes through the door

(*BRIAN's house. He is sat playing on the PS2, still in his work clothes. LEAH is smashed.*)

Leah If a tree falls in the woods is my life still shit?

Brian What?

Leah If you saw me Dad
In the club when you're looking for someone to once over
And you looked at my life
Objectively not knowing me as your daughter like
Would you see that my life is shit?

Brian What are you talking about?

Leah Is my life shit?

Brian Leah it's quarter to four I've only just got in –

Leah Answer me.

(*He puts the PS2 controller down.*)

Brian Well are ya happy?

Leah Yes. Usually.

Brian There you are then. Ya life's fine. Go to bed.

(*He picks the controller up again.*)

Leah You're not answering the question.
Is my life shit?

Brian Leah –

Leah Dad. Answer the fucking question.

(*Puts the controller down again.*)

Brian No. You're just you. You've got a job you like. You do things you like. You've got friends. You're good. Your life is fine. You're happy. What more do you want?

Leah You would say that wouldn't you.

Brian What you on about?

Leah You fucking would say that.

Brian Leah –

Leah You fucked it for me. You fucked it for me when I was a kid. You didn't get me piano lessons.

Brian Piano lessons?

Leah Well yano – anything. No lessons. Holly did. I didn't. Nothing. Or make me read –

Brian Leah

Leah It's fucking disgusting Dad.

Brian We used to read Harry Potter.

Leah No we didn't. I've only seen the films!

Brian What's happened, you were fine when you left the house?

Leah Doesn't matter.

Brian Talk to me.

Leah No.

Brian Leah –

Leah OK fine, I'll tell you what's the matter. I've spent my life paying for your mistakes.

Brian What are you on about?

Leah I could have gone to university. I could have been a nurse. I could have been rich but you fucked it before I was even born.

Holly's got a good job and money because her parents gave her everything and you gave me nothing.

Brian So it's my fault you kids want everything on a plate?

Leah Yeah it is because you fucking…ate the plate.

Brian What?

Leah You ate the plate. You fucking ate it. And you've digested it and now you're spitting bits of it back out at us. You're lending us semi-digested fucking korma and Chinese and expecting us to turn it into caviar.

Brian Alright Leah, calm down.

Leah No fuck you! Fuck you Dad. Every bad day I have is because of you. I'm fucked because you were fucking fat and lazy and too fucking sub-par to be anything other than a bouncer. And everyone laughs at you, did you know that? Everyone else's dads take the piss because you can't do anything but beat people up. They provide for their family. They work so their kids can do stuff. And you just exist. You're just alive. Not for me. Just to survive. You don't read. You don't think. All you've done is fuck me up. And I've had enough. What's the point in you? Why do you even get up in the morning? Why are you alive?

Brian You're drunk. I'm going to bed. Happy Birthday Leah.

(BRIAN gives LEAH her birthday present and goes off to bed. She opens it. It's a new Apple iPhone that he's had to save up for. LEAH feels guilty.)

> Drifting away
> We're drifting apart
> We used to be closer way back when
> I'm ready to soar without you near

(She takes out her LG Chocolate mobile and phones HOLLY.)

Holly Hello?

Leah Have you gone to bed?

Holly No babe, we're still partying at mine.

Leah I want that job.

Holly Alright. Cool. You coming round?

Leah Yeah. Fuck it. I'm coming round.

(She leaves.)

(The rain falls, the sound of the ASTEROID creeps back in.)

The MC The rivers flood into Hull

And soon The Avenues are full of water and all of the sons and daughters of the city are full of pity for the people whose houses got dragged under

And for a second

Everyone feels alive

But it's not long before the cycle takes over.

Even Asteroids get bored of cycles

Our Asteroid can see that even though it seems like everyone's swimming

Really they're drowning and they're taking the world with them.

TRACK 10: "STOP THE WORLD"

The Asteroid

*Stop the world
You need to get off.
For the birds and the bees
You need to get off.
Stop the world
You need to get off.
For the stars and the seas
You need to get off.
Stop the world
You need to get off.
Your world is rotting
From the outside in
And the ice is wearing thin.
The stars aren't beautiful
When you never look up.
And beauty can't move you
When your feet are stuck.
Stop the world you need to get off
Stop the world before its too late
Stop the world you need to get off
Stop the world your dreams are done.*

Three

Saturday 24th June 2017

(Ten years pass. The sights and sounds of Broken Britain give way to a more electronic, digital world. Donald Trump is President of the United States and Theresa May is negotiating Britain's exit from the EU… We are now in 2017's Brexit Britain.)

The MC Another ten years pass. The moon circles the earth three thousand six hundred and fifty times, each time more turbulent than the last. It's 2017 in Brexit Britain and Hull is the UK City of Culture. Blades, blue people and belief. Right, now take your phones out and film me, film me. Let's do this!

> *Woah woah*
> *We're doing what we want to*
> *Woah woah*
> *And no one's gonna stop us*
> *Woah woah*
> *We're fucking immortal*
> *And we're not going anywhere*
> *We're not going anywhere*

(We see the 2017 versions of CHRIS and LEAH, on their smartphones. They look older.)

Chris finishes his degree, but unfortunately for him he does not do it that spectacularly

He doesn't become a psychologist

But he does become something his contemporaries take the piss out of when they're pissed

Chris becomes a councillor.

Who once helped a woman feel better after a stranger pounced on her

He also fell in love

Not with anyone he'd want to fall in love with
But with someone who loved him despite the fact he's a div. He married Carly. A woman with such fragility and mediocrity she thought Chris loving her was an act of chivalry.

And she does that because no one's needed her the way Chris does -

At some point average Chris and average Carly have an average kid called Collin

Who's fine enough, they think

Chris loves Collin

Collin gives him meaning

And he's A Good Dad.

But there's nothing special about Collin, much like there was nothing special about Chris
So, to prevent Collin from making the same mistake of wishing and scheming Chris discourages Collin from dreaming

Chris is happy

            That's the important thing.

                Woah woah
            We're doing what we want to
                Woah woah
            And no one's gonna stop us
                Woah woah
            We're fucking immortal
            And we're not going anywhere
            We're not going anywhere

On the other side of Hull, Leah has found her fortune - but at what cost?

Just because she's rich doesn't mean she's fine

She sells energy to companies and from time to time she bullshits.

They could google it
                And Leah knows

But Leah is more in love with the idea of people seeing her be rich than she is with the idea of being kind.

She puts pictures on Facebook of her in nice cars

Clubs

Champagne

And occasionally

but only occasionally

She tags her best friend and colleague Holly Moffit in them by "mistake" to help bury the rage where she can't see it.
Also when she's feeling particularly brash she tags her buddies from Build-a-Bear in the hope they'll shit themselves with jealousy.

She's obsessed with the idea that people thought she'd failed and is determined to show how she overcame it all to live the life of luxury.

Our heroes are still not looking above their heads.

At the giant fucking asteroid that has seen the hatefulness of humanity and has decided it's destiny is to obliterate it completely, like a distant cousin did to the dinosaurs. Probably. She wants to put an end to the selfishness. The trouble. And give Earth a chance to build itself back up from the rubble.

TRACK 11b: "TONIGHT WE DIE"

The Asteroid

The human race
Is run
The time to start again
Has come.
Has come.
Has come.
Tonight
You die.
Tonight
We die.
Tonight
You die.
Tonight
We die.
Tonight
You die.
Tonight
You die.
Tonight
We die.

The MC The asteroid streams towards the earth.

TRACK 12: "SLEEPWALKING TO THE STARS"

Sleepwalking to the stars
Days drifting, they pass me by
Wake me up
Set me free
And let me see the morning.

(*BRIAN's house. LEAH sits, on her iPhone.*)

Leah I'm at my dads for oven baked smilies, chips and peas for my birthday.
I'd rather eat out but he pleads for some quality time
He's desperate to breathe in my success and it's fucking petty.
I'm wearing my fucking Karen Millen dress and I look good.
Fucking Holly the stupid bint WhatsApps me to tell me she's running late
Three dancing lady emojis and the monkey with its hands on its eyes
It's starting to rain from Hull's grey skies
I've got a nightmare that it'll ruin my velvet shoes, it's driving me insane.

(*BRIAN appears holding a homemade birthday cake.*)

Brian I made a cake to celebrate, darling.

Leah Oh, none of that no.

Brian But I made it.

Leah I don't want carbs Dad!

Brian There's no need to be so nasty.

Leah Fuck off Dad.

Brian Alright.
I'll throw it in the bin then.
Are you staying here or at yours?

Leah Mine.

Brian Ok.
Well, nice to have you round for tea.
I'll put this cake in the fridge and eat it tomorrow
Night.

Leah Yeah.
Night.

Brian Be safe.

Leah I will.

Brian Love you.

Leah Yeah alright.

Brian Love you.

Leah Yeah Dad I fucking love you too. Alright.

Brian I'm trying my best.

Leah I'm lending you money regardless, you don't have to be weird to earn it.

Brian I'm just being nice.

Leah No one's just nice. Not my fault no one wants an old bouncer; there's no need to be all weird.

Brian Alright. Happy Birthday.

Leah And as he turns to exit he picks up the Mail to read the latest on Brexit
The doorbell rings; the sound of my one and only mate

(The doorbell rings.)

Holly Sorry I'm late

Leah You're taking the piss it's my birthday.

Holly I know, sorry babes
I went to ya flat.

Leah You were late this morning as well.

Holly I'm sorry.
Right let's do lines.

(They do some lines.)

Sleepwalking to the stars
Days drifting, they pass me by
Wake me up
Set me free
And let me see the morning.

YOU ROCK!
Hope we get some cock!

Leah The truth is I don't want to be going out
I'm too old to get me tits out and pout
I just want to feel like I'm living that life I never lived.

Holly I've got to be back before 1.

Leah Why?

Holly I've got a Tinder shag lined up.

Leah Fucking hell.
I just want a friend tonight.
Can't you be a fucking friend and not try and get cock on my birthday?

Holly I've got other things to do.

Leah For fuck's sake.
I just want a fucking mate.
Not a date.
I can get anything I want
Anything
Films
Clothes
Books
What ever
Just by moving my finger
Anything except for relationships that linger.

Holly Shall we get fucked?

Leah Yes Holly.
Yes let's get fucked
And find something to fill this void
Or just forget about it for a bit.

Here's to you getting shagged
And me stopping thinking for a bit
And we'll both go out
And go home.
Feeling
What ever
Come on let's get a selfie

(They take selfies, smiling and pouting – pretending to have the best time ever – and then leave the house.)

(CHRIS' house. CHRIS looks older, wearing a nostalgic 90s t-shirt.)

> *Sleepwalking to the stars*
> *Days drifting, pass me by*
> *Wake me up*
> *Set me free*
> *And let me see the morning.*

The MC Older

Balder

Wiser

Chris feeds his little kid some Tizer fizzing at the brim like lava.

(KIMBERLEY comes in singing Happy Birthday, holding a bag of presents.)

Chris Thanks. Have you cleaned in here?

Kimberley Yeah.

Chris Why you done that?

Kimberley Just thought you could use some help.

Chris This is like your flat.

Kimberley I thought that's how you liked it.

Chris Carly's going to go mental. Stop controlling me!

(CHRIS starts getting changed into a banana costume. KIMBERLEY doesn't bat an eyelid.)

Kimberley Got you a present.

Chris What is it?

(He opens it. A bottle of anti-ageing moisturiser, some scales and a Teach Yourself Mandarin book.)

Chris What the fuck Mum? Anti-ageing moisturiser? Scales? Mandarin?

Kimberley I thought you could start looking after yourself. Learn a language and maybe you can get a good job, earn some money. Give your children a chance to be somebody. Like I did for you. Even if you did fuck it up.

Chris Oh for fuck's sake. You should get a boyfriend.

Kimberley Why?

Chris Then he can take all this shit.

Kimberley I don't want one

Chris Yeah well be happy then – stop taking your misery out on me.

Kimberley Ok. It's alright for you with ya job and ya wife and ya kid – your whole life ahead of you – I haven't got any of that.

Chris I'm your kid!

Kimberley Then act like it. I'm old and alone. Be a son. Don't talk to me like I'm a hindrance. I gave you everything.

Chris Yeah, well thank you very much. That worked out well didn't it.

Kimberley I'm going to get changed into my pyjamas.
You ready for your birthday party?

Chris Yes. Obviously. I wouldn't dress like this if I wasn't.

(COLLIN comes in, laughs at his dad's costume.)

Kimberley Have you done your homework?

Collin Yes. I'm eight.

Kimberley Good boy.
See he's bright
He'll do fine.
He reminds me of a son of mine.
Once upon a time.

Chris Except he'll be happy.
I hope.

Kimberley And are you not?

Chris You getting ready?

Kimberley Where is Carly?

The MC Carly is the woman he met in Spiders with terrible athletes foot
She has a crippling anxiety about her feet the poor hen
And as a result can't talk to men.
Chris pounced on it.
Her insecurity gives him security.
Despite the fact he doesn't love her.
He's making do and so is she.

Chris Book club

Kimberley All night?

Chris We just needed a break.

Kimberley Why?

Chris It's hard to spend a long time with one person.

Kimberley Ok.
I understand.
I'm just going to go and get ready.

(She leaves.)

Collin How come you and Mummy don't ever hold hands?

Chris Do you want some more of your book?

Collin She always wants to hold hands but you don't let her.

Chris We've got five minutes before I need to go, do you want a bit of your book?

Collin Are you in love?

Chris Yes. Of course we are.

Collin When you're at work do you think about Mummy?

Chris Yes.

Collin What do you think?

Chris I think how good she'd be at my job.

Collin Because she's just a claims expert.

Chris Don't say just. I think she's a good listener so she'd be good at counselling.
Do you want some more of Harry Potter?

Collin Did you never want to be rich?

Chris Enough questions Collin. Do you want some more Harry Potter?

Collin Yes.

Chris Ok.
Harry knew that Voldemort –

Collin I want to be a bad guy.

Chris What?

Collin When I'm older I want to be a bad guy.

Chris What do you mean?

Collin Bad guys get everything they want don't they.

Chris What do you mean?

Collin Like the President.

Chris What does he have that you want?

Collin Women and money. Being away from the Muslims.

Chris Collin.

Collin What?

Chris That's –
Where did you hear that?

Collin Dunno.
Just heard it.

Chris You can't say that.

Collin Why?

Chris Because in this family
We're all about love and understanding
We care about as many people as possible being happy
Ok?

Collin Yeah I agree with that.

Chris Ok

Collin As long as I'm happy first.

Chris We've all got to be happy.

Collin Nanny said 'if I can dream it, I can do it'

Chris She shouldn't say that.

Collin Why not?

Chris Because the world doesn't work like that. And also R. Kelly's shit.

Collin Who's R. Kelly?

Chris Doesn't matter.

Collin Are you going out tonight?

Chris I am

Collin Where are you going?

Chris To my birthday party.

Collin I want you to stay in

Chris Ok.

Collin So you're being selfish.

Chris You're eight!

Collin I'm just saying
Can I play on the iPad?

Chris Yeah. *(He gives him the iPad.)*

(KIMBERLEY comes down in jimmy jammies.)

Kimberley Right let's get you ready for bed. Put that down.
(She takes the iPad off him.)

Chris I've got to go.
Collin –

Collin Yeah?

Chris Do you remember when you fell down the stairs and banged your knee?

Collin Yeah.

Chris What did I do?

Collin You rubbed it better.

Chris What did you need me to do?

Collin Be kind to me.

Chris Everyone needs that Collin. All the time. Don't forget how you felt. Everyone needs kindness. Be kind, always be kind.

Collin Happy Birthday Daddy. I made you a present.

(COLLIN hands CHRIS a picture of him. It's mummy looking glamorous. CHRIS looks fat and smelly.)

Chris Is this how you see me?

Collin Yes. I did this too.

(It's a picture saying 'I WILL NEVER GET MARRIED, BE POOR AND SAD LIKE YOU'. And COLLIN lying a big double bed alone, happy with loads of money and women.)

Chris Goodnight Collin.

TRACK 13: "EVERYTHING ECHOING"

> *Everything*
> *Everything*
> *Everything Echoing*
> *Everything*
> *Everything*
> *Everything Echoing*
> *Round and round and round and round*
> *My head, my heart, my hands, my home*
> *Round and round and round and round*
> *I never thought I'd be alone*
> *My head, my heart, my hands, my home*
> *Them and us, you and me*
> *I never thought I'd be alone*

The MC They step out

Out onto the chewing gum spangled pavements

Out into the night

Out into the potential for fucking or fun or a fight.

The night.

The last night

And although, for a few hours a week, they live like it

They don't know this time it's real.

An asteroid is heading right for them to reduce the world to rubble and steel.

Human lullabies and legends have no function now and they cannot feel

That these are their last moments

The last things to grab onto

And that's it.

These are our last moments

This is how we die

Chris Tom's wearing a hot dog costume

Leah Holly doesn't even look at me anymore.

Chris I'm standing in the taxi rank next to a giant hot dog

Leah Let's put vodka in coke bottles like we're fourteen again.

Holly Why?

Leah Because I want to be young again.
Please.
For one night.

Holly Fine.

Chris And I'm dressed like a banana.

Leah She's got an attitude problem.

Chris I've got a kid.

Leah Why won't ya stay out with me?

Chris I don't want to be going out with a big hot dog.

Leah Why are you leaving me for a man?

Chris I don't want to be dressed as a banana.

Leah Go home.

Chris I'm not having a line.

Leah Seriously fuck off.

Chris No.

Leah FUCK OFF HOLLY.

Chris No.
Ok.

Leah I'm alive

Chris I hate this

Leah I just need to

Chris I'm just going for a walk.

(He takes off his banana costume and throws it.)

Leah I just need to be alone with my thoughts.

Chris I'm thinking I'm not like you and I never have been and I wish that I'd got out of this.

Leah She left.

Chris I walk out.

Leah I'm alone

Chris The stars look big

Leah The worst thing is that I'd do it to her.

Chris I don't like any of them

Leah For the validation

Chris I did

Leah To feel accepted by someone.

Chris But I'm a dad now.

Leah That's all there is

Chris I've never liked this.

Leah Validation

Chris My purpose

Leah I just want people to like me

Chris I –

Leah It's –

Chris Ah –

Leah –

Chris I –

Leah Ah –

Chris I –

Leah –

> *Everything*
> *Everything*
> *Everything Echoing*
> *Everything*
> *Everything*
> *Everything Echoing*
> *Round and round and round and round*
> *My head, my heart, my hands, my home*
> *Round and round and round and round*
> *I never thought I'd be alone*
> *My head, my heart, my hands, my home*
> *Them and us, you and me*
> *I never thought I'd be alone*

(They both have panic attacks, the music mocks them.)

(CHRIS crumbles.)

(LEAH sucks it up.)

(CHRIS gets up. Breathes.)

Chris Fuck it.

Leah I'm going dancing.

The MC As they dance they can't see The Asteroid falling

All they can hear is the 4 4 beat running through the veins of the club.

Leah here alone

Chris here with his mates all married and grown up.

Either side of the dance floor

The rhythm of a bass drum pounding through them

The booze and the loneliness making their eyes scout for a connection with a stranger

They see each other

And a memory flickers through their minds

Something about hope

And ambition

And life

And love

But neither of them know what it is

Neither of them can quite put their finger on this feeling of familiarity towards each other.

And all they can see is the flashing lights of the DJ and the girls trying too hard to be girls and the boys trying too hard to be boys.

They're lost here. And they know it.

Too old to be in this place.

Too lonely not to be.

Figures from each other's past serving as a reminder of a life that was never lived.

Leah Are you a psychologist?

Chris Sort of. Not really. No. You a vet?

Leah Nowhere near.

The MC The asteroid screams closer to the earth.

Leah In whispered voices in the clubs darkest corner we confess to each other the unbearable weight of the enormity of existing. I see him, tied by the shackles of being told he could be anything but discovering he's average, well up with tears in his drink puffy eyes.

The MC Desperate to destroy the hate, the jealousy, the selfishness, the greed, the inequality, the ego the…everything. It notices for the first time, through the fog of badness, the tiny acts of beauty. It notices the carers, the paramedics, the charities, the random acts of kindness… The actual beauty of the world. All the things our heroes forget, all the things they miss with their passing eye.

Chris I see her, shimmering with everything money can buy but possessing nothing close to love. We tell each other how we hate that our bodies aren't good enough

Leah That our hair isn't perfect enough

Chris That we're not clever enough. How we hate that we won't own homes. Our shit jobs. Our lack of savings.

Leah The stress.

Chris The stress.

Leah The stress.

The MC And for a second the asteroid decides it's not worth it. For a second it doesn't want to die. And it thinks that maybe it shouldn't do this.

Chris We talk of our plastic lives; white teeth and wide smiles that make the wound deeper. Of how we can't LIVE. We can't DO ANYTHING real, because we're too busy buying stuff and selling ourselves.

The MC But it's too late.

Leah We talk about how our wars don't feel real, our relationships don't feel real, even the hate and the anger and the jealousy and the bitterness DON'T FEEL REAL. The only thing that feels real is the lack of love in our worlds. The lack of compassion, of kindness, of truth.

The MC She crashes into the earth at a speed greater than any of us can imagine, with the force of a billion trains.

Chris And in the corner of the room, in the lights and the sound and the people and the darkness, we tell each other that we were happier in simpler times.

Leah In building bears and playing with friends.

Chris In dream walls and Union Jack dresses.

The MC The sea drifts in.

Leah And he says it'll be worse for his kid. Inheriting fear and loathing in Hull. Because that, he says, is all he'll leave behind; fear of other people and the loathing of himself.

Chris And she says she doesn't want kids because she has nothing to offer them. Because it's selfish. Because she doesn't want them to feel the shame that she feels.

The MC The shores recede.

Chris We say we wish we were our parents.

Leah We wish we were our parents.

Together We wish we were our parents.

Kimberley And, us, their parents sit, alone, wishing we were our children.

Brian Wishing we were our children.

Together Wishing we were our children.

Kimberley & Brian (underscoring...)
Everything
Everything
Everything Echoing
Everything
Everything
Everything Echoing
Round and round and round and round
My head, my heart, my hands, my home
Round and round and round and round
I never thought I'd be alone
My head, my heart, my hands, my home
Them and us, you and me
I never thought I'd be alone

The MC The people of the Earth stand on the coasts and look out at the horizon; the shipwrecks and corpses and buried treasures of the ocean being exposed for the first time

Leah And after we say all of this, we laugh.

Chris Because we can't do anything else.

Leah We laugh and we laugh and we laugh.

Chris Because we don't laugh much anymore and it's fucking funny.

The MC And then the dust travels. A cloud spectre of dust rising taller than anything man has seen. Like a smog it travels across the globe and it hangs in the air over towns and cities and it creeps through windows and into houses and into pubs

Leah We want everything and nothing at the same time.

Chris We want to be rich, and hard done by, and interesting, and clever, and kind, and funny…

Leah …and sexy, and loved, and right, and left, and

Chris and

Leah and

Chris and

Leah and

Chris and we want everyone to know we exist

Leah and to appreciate us

Chris and to like us

Leah and to love us

Chris and we want it all instantly

Leah and we want everything

Chris everything

Leah everything

Together everything everything everything

(*They repeat the word 'everything' until they can't speak no more.*)

The MC In the club the two bodies sit, unaware of the chaos, exhausted by their own truth like two lovers that have spent the night ravishing each other. They're empty. The weight is gone from their shoulders. They're free. And for the first time in a long time they feel content. Like life is now for living. And, feeling closer in this moment than she's ever felt to another human, she turns to him, in the light and the sound and says…

Leah Do you want to go and look at the stars?

The MC And they do

They step out

And look at the sky

And they see it

The burning fire

Screaming towards them

And in that second

That one second

They see the life they should have lived

The one that was moment to moment

The one that wasn't lost in getting things

Achieving

The one where they stood and breathed

And connected with other humans

Where they stopped dreaming

And started living

And if they knew that then

If they knew that then

They might not have been regretting it all so much as they die.

The Asteroid
Everything
Everything
Everything Echoing
Everything
Everything
Everything Echoing
Round and round and round and round
Your head, your heart, your hands, your home
Round and round and round and round
You never thought you'd be alone
Your head, your heart, your hands, your home
Round and round and round and round
You never thought you'd be alone

(The ASTEROID comes into focus.)

As the universe is clogged with people screaming what they would have done differently, humanity dies.

The earth is empty.

Life is dead.

And all that's left are the towers that were built to show off wealth. And they're nothing without people in them.

There is nothing but silence.
And the dust.
And the land stretching out for ever.

And now we, together in this club, can see it in the fire and the destruction. That there is no need for this bullshit. That all we have to do is make it count right NOW. Forget about how well you're doing, look up and LIVE with spirit in your heart. Stand up for kindness and joy and hope. Stand up for each other. Sing your song so loudly that the whole world can hear it. Live your life. I fucking dare you.

The MC
I won't let the bastards grind me down
Won't let this world fuck me up
I won't give in and I will speak out
And in my dreams I'll dream of dancing
So we're gonna dance for all our friends tonight
We're gonna dance for all our families too
Tonight
I'm gonna live for now
For tonight
There's nothing we can't change

All
So we're gonna dance for all our friends tonight
We're gonna dance for all our families too
Tonight
We're gonna live for now
For tonight
There's nothing we can't change

MC
Let's dance tonight, let's dance and dance
In peace and love let's dance and let's dance
(The rest of the instruments join in, it's big and fun - a protest song)

All
So we're gonna dance for all our friends tonight
We're gonna dance for all our families too
Tonight
We're gonna live for now
For tonight
There's nothing we can't change

End.

Scores

James Frewer / Luke Barnes / Paul Smith

THEATRE THAT MAKES A NOISE

Act 1 - Prologue - 1987 // Our Heroes Are Born

Luke Barnes / Paul Smith

James Frewer

With an air of tight trousered campness

♩ = 122

I wan-na dance with some-bod- y, 'cos noth-ings gun-na stop us now,_ there's

no such thing as so - ci - ety, And heav-en is a place on earth,_____

Act 1 - Track 1b - We Sing For You (Prologue)

Luke Barnes / Paul Smith

James Frewer

Euphoric as Fuck

♩ = 80 ish

We sing for you,_ We sing_ for you, We sing for you__ and the stars are sing-ing too. For your

bea - ting hearts are beau-ti - ful__ there's noth -ing you can't do,_____

Act 1 - Track 2a - 1997 Intro Cool Britannia

Luke Barnes / Paul Smith

James Frewer

A hint of Manc

♩ = 145 ish

Bar-bie girls, Bee-tle bums, More mon-ey and more prob lems, I bel-ieve I can fly,

I be-leive I can fly, believe I can fly,

be – lieve I can fly, believe I can fly.

Act 1 - Track 2b - Things Can Only Get Better

Luke Barnes / Paul Smith

James Frewer

Sad but never morbid

♩ = 75

Our An-ces-tors are watch-ing, as we burn our fires, Brigh-ter than what came be-fore,

brigh-ter than they ev - er saw, they say things can on-ly get bet-ter things can on-ly get bet-ter

things can on-ly get bet-ter they say. Our An-ces-tors are list-'ning Their ghosts are in the walls,

tel-ling us all to rise up and to take our place in the stars. They say things can on ly get bet-ter,

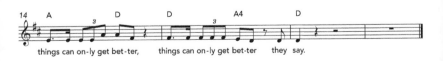

things can on-ly get bet-ter, things can on-ly get bet-ter they say.

Act 1 - Track 3 - You and Me

Luke Barnes / Paul Smith

James Frewer

90s Haze with a hint of emotion

♩. = 110

Act 1 - Track 4 - Watch The Sun Together

Luke Barnes / Paul Smith

James Frewer

Tender

♩ = 84

Just let me in, let me in, let us dance for tom - mor__ ow. Oh let me

in, let me in, let's watch the sun to - ge - ther.

Act 1 - Track 5 - Wake Up When Dreams Are Over

Luke Barnes / Paul Smith

James Frewer

Foreboding

♩ = 88

There's noth-ing left but sleep now just dark-ness in the dark. There's no-one left to hear now, the

stars shine in the park. Hearts wake up when dreams are ov - er,

hearts wake up when dreams are done, hearts wake up when dreams are ov - er,

hearts wake up when dreams are done.

Act 2 - Track 6 - 2007 Our Time Has Come

Luke Barnes / Paul Smith

James Frewer

Look Into The Sun Directly

♩ = 165

Starz in our eyes so

shut up and drive, with all my friends, time to pre-tend. What's done is done and la da da,_ our

time has come ah ha ha ha, what's done is done and la da da,_ our time has come ah

ah ha ha, Cheal sea daggers and paper planes, big girls don't cry, you're so nai - ve. What's

done is done and la da da,_ our time has come ah ha ha ha. what's

done is done and la da da,_ our time has come ah ah ha ha,

Act 2 - Track 6b - I Dream Of You

Luke Barnes / Paul Smith

James Frewer

Musing

♩ = 94

Act 2 - Track 7 - Rainbows, Spiders, Vultures

Luke Barnes / Paul Smith

James Frewer

Tempo di Fuck You Up

♩ = 84

Act 2 - Track 8 - Night Falls

Luke Barnes / Paul Smith

James Frewer

Glastonbury Moment

♩ = 190

Night falls,__ save__ me.__ Night falls,__ hold__

me.___ Let me in your arms when night falls, I just wan-na be free. I can feel your

charms when night falls, to geth-er we'll be free. Fall with me._____

Act 2 - Track 9 - Drifting Away

Luke Barnes / Paul Smith

James Frewer

Diverging and Swerving

♩ = 100

Drif- ting___ a - way, we're drif- ting___ a - part, we used to be clos - er

way back___ when. I'm rea - dy to soar,___ with - out you___ near.___

Act 2 - Track 10 - Stop The World

Luke Barnes / Paul Smith

James Frewer

Angry

♩ = 90

Am / Em / F / C / D / Am

Stop the wo-rld,_ you need to get off. For the birds and the bees you need to get off._

5 Am / Em / F / C / D / Am

Stop the wo-rld,_ you need to get off. For the stars and the seas you need to get off._

9 Am / Em / F / C / G

Stop the wo - rld,_ you need to get off. Your world is ro-tting from the out-side in and the

12 Em / Am / G / Am / Em / F

ice is wear-ing thin._ The stars aren't beau-ti - ful when you nev-er look up,_ and

15 G / Am / Em / F / Am / Em

beau-ty can't move you when your feet_ are stuck. Stop the world you need to get off,

18 F / C / Am / Em

stop the world be - fore it's too late, stop the world you need to get off,

20 F / C

stop the world your dreams are done.

©JamesFrewer

Act 3 - Track 11a - We're Not Going Anywhere

Luke Barnes / Paul Smith

James Frewer

Millennial Shite.

♩ = 195

Wo-ah, wo-ah, we're do-ing what we want to. Wo-ah, wo-ah, and no things gon-na stop us.

Wo - ah, wo - ah, we're fu-cking im-mor - tal, we're not go-ing a - ny where,

We're not go - ing a - ny- where.___

Act 3 - Track 11b - Tonight We Die

Luke Barnes / Paul Smith

James Frewer

Techno Morrissey

♩ = 130

Act 3 - Track 12 - Sleep Walking To The Stars

Luke Barnes / Paul Smith

James Frewer

Hypnotic

♩ = 78

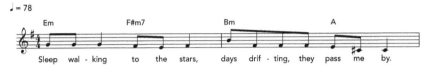

Sleep   wal - king   to   the   stars,   days   drif - ting,   they   pass   me   by.

Wake   me   up,   set   me   free   and   let   me   see   the   mor - ning.___

Act 3 - Track 13 - Everything Echoing

Luke Barnes / Paul Smith

James Frewer

Fucking Epic

♩. = 60

Ev-ery - thing, ev - ery -thing, ev-ery -thing, ec-ho-ing. Ev-ery-thing, ev-ery -thing, ev-ery -thing, ec - ho ing.

Round and round and round and round, my

head, my heart, my hands, my home. Round and round and round and round, I

never thought I'd be a - lone.____ My head, my heart, my

hands, my home. Them and us,_____ you and me.__ I

nev - er thought I'd be a - lone.__

Act 3 - Track 14 - Anthem

Luke Barnes / Paul Smith

James Frewer

Banger

♩ = 80

I won't let the bas-tards grind me down, I won't let the world fuck me up. I

won't give in and I will speak out and in my dreams I'll dream of dan- cing. We're gun-na dance for

all our friends to-night, We're gun-na dance for all our fam-ilies too, to- night,_____ we're

gun-na live for now, to- night,___ there's no-thing we can't change. Let's dance to -night, let's dance and

dance. In peace and love we dance and we dance. We're gun-na dance for

all our friends to-night, We're gun-na dance for all our fam-ilies too, to -

night,_____ we're gun-na live for now, to- night,_____ there's no-thing we can't change.